THINK BIG

THE GREATEST IDEAS IN CONSERVATION

IZZI HOWELL

Cavendish Square

Published in 2026 by Cavendish Square Publishing, LLC
2544 Clinton Street, Buffalo, NY 14224

First published in Great Britain in 2022 by Wayland

Website: cavendishsq.com

Author and editor: Izzi Howell
Designer: Clare Nicholas

The publisher would like to thank the following for permission to reproduce their pictures:
Alamy: Everett Collection Inc 11b; Getty: THEPALMER cover bottom, nelik 4b, Megan Brady 6l, Monty Fresco/Stringer 8, ssuaphoto 9b, Julian Wasser/The LIFE Images Collection 12, JOYCE NALTCHAYAN/AFP 13r, Tim Rue/Bloomberg 22t, ilbusca 22b, lgphotography 25b, Graphic_BKK1979 29t; Global Diversity Crop Trust: 19t and 19b; Library of Congress: LC-USZ62-44164 DLC 6r; NASA: NASA/NOAA 16b, NASA's Goddard Space Flight Center 17b; The Ocean Cleanup: 20b, 21t and 21b; Our World in Data: CAIT Climate Data Explorer via. Climate Watch 24b; Shutterstock: Joseph Sohm cover top, 13l and 17t, Kodda 4t, Menno Schaefer, Andrew Sutton, GUDKOV ANDREY and Harry Collins Photography 5l, s_bukley 5r, Marion Smith – Byers 7t, SergeUWPhoto 7b, VectorMine 9t, Grindstone Media Group 10t, Paul Reeves Photography 10b, PhotocechCZ 14t, SERGEI PRIMAKOV 15t, Yvdalmia 15c, Adalbert Dragon 15b, Narin C 16t, Rich Carey 20t, Nasky 23t, Fly_and_Dive 23b, a katz 24t, Ryan Rodrick Beiler 25t, Mike Jett 26t, Per Grunditz 26b and 31, Holli 27, Dalibor Danilovic 28, MikeDotta 29c, divedog and Danuta 29b, Alfmaler 31.

All design elements from Shutterstock.

Every attempt has been made to clear copyright. Should there be any inadvertent omission, please apply to the publisher for rectification.

Cataloging-in-Publication Data
Names: Howell, Izzi.
Title: The greatest ideas in conservation / Izzi Howell.
Description: Buffalo, New York : Cavendish Square Publishing, 2026. |
Series: Think big | Includes index, glossary, and bibliographic information
Identifiers: ISBN 9781502675279 (pbk) | ISBN 9781502675286 (library bound) |
ISBN 9781502675293 (ebook)
Subjects: LCSH: Climate Change—Juvenile Literature |
Conservation of Natural Resources--Juvenile Literature |
Environmental protection—Juvenile Literature
Classification: LCC GE195.5 H69 2026 | DDC 333.72 --dc25

CPSIA compliance information: Batch #CS26CSQ: For further information contact Cavendish Square Publishing LLC at 1-877-980-4450.

Printed in the United States of America

Find us on

Contents

Conservation

The need to protect the environment has been getting a lot of media attention recently, but conservation is not a new idea. Over the past 150 years, many great minds have come up with brilliant ideas to help save the natural world.

Coal power plants release greenhouse gases that contribute to global warming.

Where Do We Begin?

For most of human history, the population of Earth was so low that people did not have a serious negative impact on the environment. However, since the Industrial Revolution (c.1760–1900), human activity has been damaging our planet in almost every way: destroying natural habitats, driving animals to extinction, consuming natural resources, and polluting the planet with greenhouse gases and waste.

Thinking Big

Some big ideas have already helped prevent a great deal of damage to the natural world. Conservation projects have stopped the extinction of many animal species, such as the giant panda, and have protected important natural habitats. Laws and clever inventions have vastly improved air and water quality in many areas.

In the 1980s, only a few hundred giant pandas remained in the wild. Thanks to habitat conservation and breeding programs in zoos, there are now over 1,800 wild giant pandas, mostly living in wildlife reserves.

THINK BIG!

Research some other species that were saved from extinction in the 20th century, such as the:

sea otter

blue whale

Siberian tiger

peregrine falcon

What put them at risk of extinction? What was done to save them? Then research an animal that is currently endangered. Which approaches could be used to protect this animal?

GENIUS

Activist Professor Wangari Maathai (1940–2011) was the founder of the Green Belt Movement in Kenya. Her organization encouraged local people, particularly women, to plant trees. This simple step solved many environmental problems – reducing deforestation, restoring habitats, and providing sustainable income for local people. Since 1977, the Green Belt Movement has planted over 51 million trees in Kenya. Maathai was awarded the Nobel Peace Prize in 2004 for her work.

National Parks

A national park is a natural area that is protected by the government. Yellowstone National Park in the west of the USA became the first national park when it was set up in 1872.

The Big Idea

In a national park, the entire ecosystem, including the landscape, animals, and plants, is protected from human activity. Construction, transportation, farming, and consumption of natural resources are banned or severely limited.

Yellowstone National Park is home to one of the largest herds of American bison and many thermal springs.

GENIUS

Ferdinand Hayden (1829–1887) was an American geologist who was part of the team that surveyed the area that would become Yellowstone National Park. Hayden was concerned that the rapidly expanding railway network would threaten this beautiful natural area. He wrote a report suggesting that it should be protected, which persuaded then U.S. President Ulysses S. Grant to turn it into a national park.

This photo of natural hot springs in Yellowstone was taken on Hayden's trip. Photos such as this helped to convince the president of the need to protect the site.

How Does It Work?

National parks are run by the government. Tax money and revenue from the park are used to pay for park maintenance and to hire staff to monitor the area. National parks can have controlled areas for special projects, such as reintroducing species. The animals are protected in these areas and can establish themselves there.

Park rangers in the Masai Mara National Reserve in Kenya are responsible for protecting species from poachers. These rangers are treating an elephant that was attacked by poachers.

Where Did It Lead?

The first U.S. national parks inspired governments around the world to create their own parks, in countries such as Canada, the UK, Japan, and Brazil. As of 2020, around 15 percent of land and around 7.6 percent of the world's oceans are protected areas.

This hawksbill turtle and coral are found in the marine area of the Komodo National Park in Indonesia.

THINK BIG!

Think of a natural area near where you live. What features does it have that should be protected? It could be its wildlife, plants, or landscape. Are there any rules already in place to protect this area? If not, could you send an email to your local leaders and encourage them to protect it?

Clean Air Act

Up until the 1950s, the United Kingdom (UK) suffered from terrible air pollution and smog (a combination of smoke and fog). However, a new law that was passed in 1956 helped to resolve the problem and improve air quality.

The Big Idea

Starting in the 18th century with the Industrial Revolution, the UK had become home to a huge number of coal-powered factories. The pollution released by these factories was so intense that it sometimes blocked out the Sun. In 1952, London experienced the worst air pollution ever recorded in the city. Thousands of people died from breathing issues caused by pollution and from traffic accidents brought about by poor visibility on the roads. It was clearly time for the UK to address the issue.

A traffic warden directing a bus with a flashlight during the Great Smog of 1952. Even in daylight, visibility was so poor that people could not see their feet on the ground.

GENIUS

Sir Hugh Beaver (1890–1967) was an English/South African engineer. He helped with research into the Great Smog. He advised the government on the importance of changing over to smokeless fuels, which was a key part of the Clean Air Act.

How Did It Work?

The solution was to pass a new law controlling air pollution – the 1956 Clean Air Act. It encouraged people to use fuels that did not produce smoke, such as electricity and gas. Both factories and homes had to change their fuels. At that time, many people still burned coal at home for heating and cooking. It took decades for these changes to be carried out across the UK, as many furnaces had to be replaced.

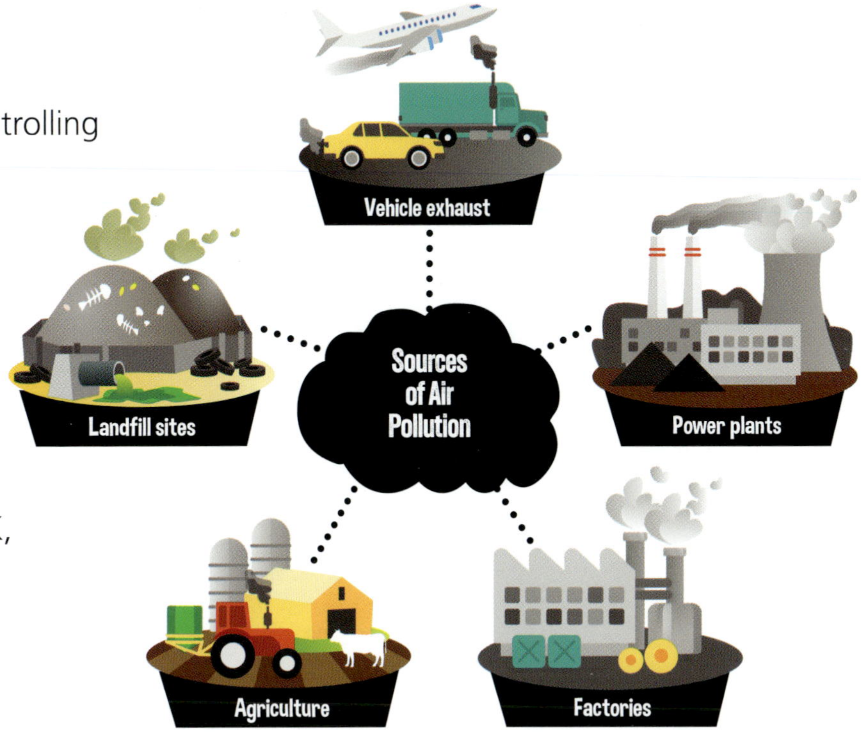

Where Did It Lead?

Although air pollution decreased greatly across the UK following the Act, it still exists today. Outside the UK, many less economically developed countries continue to use fuel that creates smoke. Around the world, air pollution kills around 7 million people a year.

Modern vehicles still release large amounts of air pollution.

THINK BIG!

What is air pollution like in your local area? Where does it come from and how could it be reduced? Think about ways of reducing car journeys and encouraging people to walk or cycle.

DDT Ban

In the mid-20th century, a new pesticide, DDT, became popular with farmers, especially in the United States. However, it quickly became clear that DDT had a devastating effect on wild animals, particularly birds. Banning DDT helped to prevent further damage and save fragile ecosystems.

The Big Idea

DDT was a very effective pesticide and so farmers were able to grow far more crops, undamaged by pests. But scientists almost immediately started noticing serious environmental consequences. Although DDT targeted insects, it was spreading through the food chain with terrible effects. Some people began to wonder if DDT should be banned.

Farmers used planes to spray DDT onto fields of crops. Huge areas were covered in the pesticide, polluting many rivers and lakes.

How Did It Work?

When DDT was sprayed on crops, there was only enough pesticide to poison and kill very small animals. However, as other animals ate the insects, and larger animals ate those animals, the amount of DDT built up in the bodies of large animals. It also washed into rivers and passed into the bodies of fish, which affected large fish-eating birds, such as bald eagles.

DDT led to bald eagles becoming endangered in North America in the 1950s and 60s. Consuming DDT made their eggshells much thinner, and so most chicks did not survive.

Where Did It Lead?

Fears concerning DDT led to a series of hearings in the United States to investigate its environmental impact. Scientists gave compelling evidence of its dangers. It was banned there in 1972. The hearings and eventual ban of DDT inspired many people to pay attention to environmental issues for the first time (see pages 12–13). However, DDT and other pesticides continue to be used worldwide, where they have a serious impact on ecosystems.

GENIUS

Rachel Carson (1907–1964) was an American marine biologist and writer. Her book *Silent Spring* raised awareness of the dangers of DDT and played a key role in motivating the U.S. government to hold the hearings that led to the DDT ban.

Rachel Carson presents information at a DDT hearing in 1963.

THINK BIG!

Organic farming doesn't use any pesticides. It is much better for the natural world, but some crops are lost to pests. Design an experiment to test yields from plants grown organically and plants grown with pesticides. How will you keep the experiment fair?

Earth Day

The release of the book *Silent Spring* and the DDT hearings created lots of interest in environmental issues in the United States. This led to the first ever Earth Day on April 22, 1970 – a mass protest to raise awareness of the importance of protecting our planet.

The Big Idea

Previously, lots of smaller environmental groups had been campaigning about separate environmental issues such as pesticide use, polluting fuels, and oil spills. All of these groups were united in one Earth Day protest. There was power in numbers and a shared message.

GENIUS

Denis Hayes (1944–) is an American environmental activist who helped to organize the first Earth Day celebration. He went on to found the Earth Day Network, which brought Earth Day to other countries, and continues to organize Earth Day events every year.

University students in California release a hot air balloon to celebrate the first Earth Day in 1970.

What Happened?

Protests and rallies took place across the United States on the first Earth Day. Around 20 million Americans took part, which at that time was 10 percent of the country's population. Earth Day celebrations continued on April 22nd every year afterward, with some focusing on specific themes, such as recycling or clean energy. Today it is one of the largest worldwide events, with over a billion people taking part.

Where Did It Lead?

Earth Day caught the public's attention and helped put pressure on the U.S. government to take environmental issues seriously. By the end of 1970, the U.S. government had set up the Environmental Protection Agency, which helped to create key laws to protect the environment. International Earth Day events help to bring together activists from around the world and highlight the importance of international cooperation.

Young people take part in a river clean-up in Los Angeles, California, to celebrate Earth Day in 1990. As well as protests, clean-up projects are often held on Earth Day.

This giant model of Earth was made to celebrate the 25th anniversary of Earth Day.

THINK BIG!

Research an environmental law in your country. What has it achieved? How could the law be changed to protect the environment further? You could think about protecting more natural spaces or species or stricter punishments for people who break the law.

Project Tiger

The Project Tiger program is a conservation success story. Through the creation of new tiger reserves and habitats, the project has managed to protect and increase the fragile Bengal tiger population in India.

Tigers usually hunt large wild animals, such as deer and buffalo, but will kill livestock if their habitat isn't big enough for them to find wild prey.

The Big Idea

India is home to most of the world's Bengal tiger population, but human activity threatens their habitat. The construction of new houses and towns cuts into tiger territories and makes it much harder for them to find enough prey. This pushes tigers into developed areas, where they are more likely to attack livestock and humans, and be killed by people. Poachers also target tigers for their fur and bones. Tiger reserves create safe spaces for tigers away from these dangers.

How Did It Work?

Project Tiger was rolled out across nine reserves in 1973 by the Indian government.

Features of Project Tiger

- Protect existing tiger habitats from further development
- Create new tiger reserves
- Relocate people from tiger territories to decrease the risk for both people and tigers alike
- Protect tigers from poachers
- Monitor tiger numbers both inside and outside reserves (35 percent of tigers live outside reserves)

Camera traps are used to monitor tiger numbers in each reserve. This is a great way to keep an eye on the tigers without disturbing them.

Where Did It Lead?

Since 1973, Project Tiger has spread to 50 reserves across India. Its protected areas cover about 2 percent of the entire country. Thanks to Project Tiger's intervention, the wild tiger population had increased to 2,967 by 2019. However, India's human population continues to grow too, and so Project Tiger must continue to expand and adapt to keep up with the needs of the tigers.

GENIUS

Project Tiger has inspired many other big cat charities around the world, such as Panthera. This organization is dedicated to preserving the habitats of all big cat species around the world, including tigers, lions, and jaguars. They partner with scientists, smaller local charities and governments to protect these animals and help increase their population.

Tigers in reserves are a huge tourist attraction, and bring in lots of money for the Indian economy. However, too much contact with humans can make tigers stressed and unhappy.

THINK BIG!

Choose another endangered animal and design your own project to protect them. What are the greatest dangers facing them? What changes could you make to protect them and their habitat? Make a poster explaining your ideas.

Ozone Hole

In 1985, scientists made a troubling discovery. Parts of the ozone layer in Earth's atmosphere above Antarctica were becoming dangerously thin. This became known as the "ozone hole." Quick thinking from scientists and governments led to a ban of the dangerous chemicals that had weakened the ozone layer.

The Big Idea

Ozone is a gas that gathers in a layer in the atmosphere 9-19 miles (15–30 km) from Earth's surface. Ozone blocks ultraviolet (UV) light from the Sun – without the ozone layer, there would be an increased risk of skin cancer in humans, among other problems.

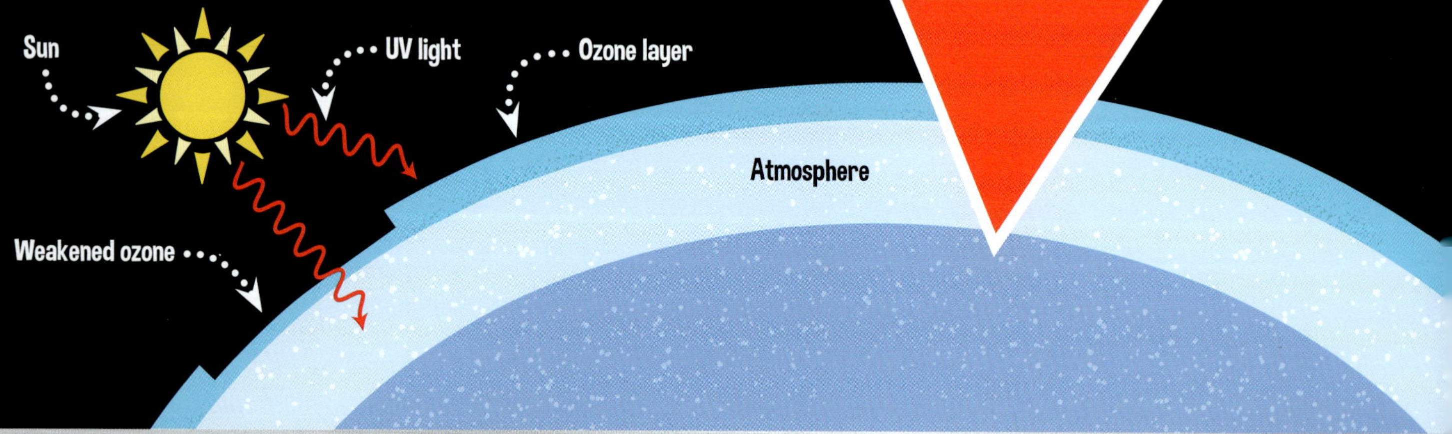

GENIUS

Jonathan Shanklin, Joe Farman, and Brian Gardiner are British meteorologists and geologists. In 1985, they were the first scientists to discover the ozone hole. They also correctly identified that chlorofluorocarbons (see page 17) were responsible for it. Later, NASA used satellites to monitor the ozone layer and confirm the scientists' research.

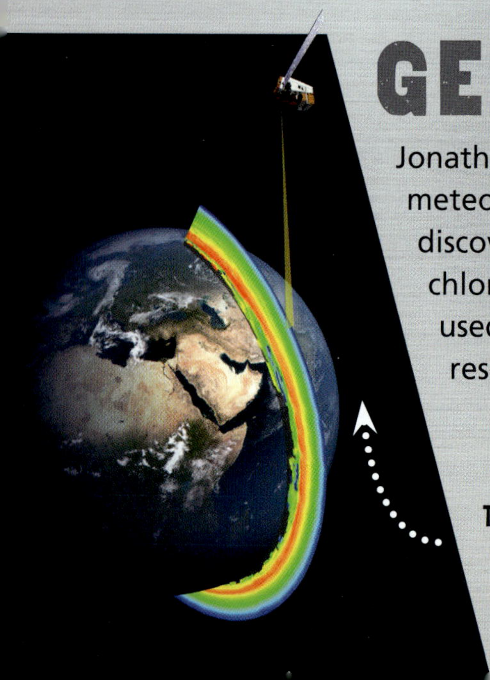

Today NASA still uses satellites to monitor and map the ozone layer. The yellow/orange color shows areas with more ozone, while blue/green areas have less ozone.

How Do CFCs Work?

Chlorofluorocarbons, or CFCs, are chemicals that break down ozone. They were widely used from the 1920s to the 1980s in fridges, air-conditioning systems, and aerosols, such as hairsprays. Once sprayed into the air, CFCs built up in the atmosphere over the South Pole due to weather conditions there. A chemical reaction between CFCs and ozone destroyed the ozone.

Aerosols containing CFCs in the 1990s. Modern aerosols do not contain CFCs.

Where Did It Lead?

The discovery that CFCs destroyed ozone led to one of the most successful environmental treaties ever – the Montreal Protocol. In 1987, every country in the United Nations signed this law banning the use of CFCs immediately. Despite the ban, the remaining CFCs in the atmosphere continued to do damage and the hole reached its largest size in the 2000s. However, thanks to the ban, the ozone layer has since stabilized and scientists hope that it will return to its pre-1950 size by the year 2080.

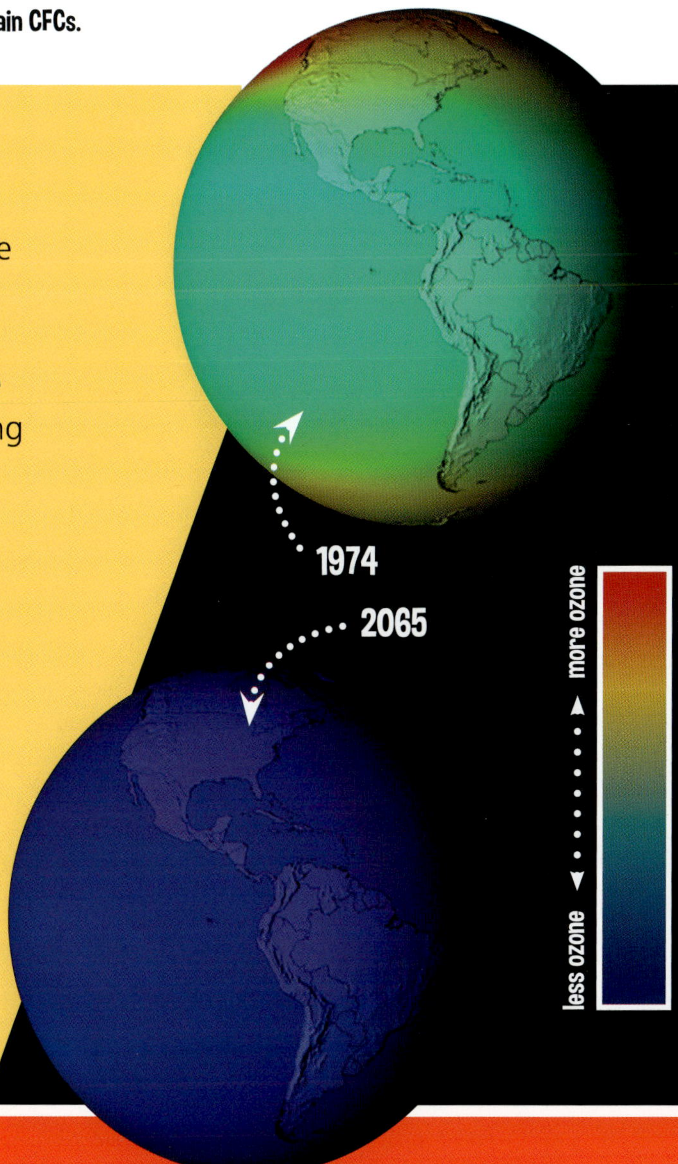

If we had continued using CFCs at the same rate, scientists believe that the ozone layer would have eventually been destroyed. This is what the ozone layer would have looked like by 2065 if the Montreal Protocol had not existed.

THINK BIG!

The Montreal Protocol was one of the most successful environmental agreements in history in that it was immediately carried out by every country. Choose another important environmental issue – what would happen if everyone around the world made immediate changes to solve the problem? What do you think would encourage people to take it more seriously?

Svalbard Global Seed Vault

The Svalbard Global Seed Vault is a seed storage facility on a remote Arctic island. It holds a huge collection of seeds from different crops. In the unlikely event that a disease or a natural catastrophe wipes out key crops and seed storage, back-ups from Svalbard would allow us to recover our food supply and biodiversity.

The Big Idea

Before Svalbard, seeds from different crop species were already stored in different seed banks around the world. However, many of these banks were vulnerable to threats, such as flooding, pests and earthquakes. A more secure seed bank was needed as the ultimate back-up.

Only the entrance to the Svalbard Global Seed Vault can be seen from the outside. The rest of the vault is hidden inside a mountain.

GENIUS

Dr. Cary Fowler (1949–) is an American agriculturalist who played an important role in the creation of the Svalbard Global Seed Vault. He suggested its remote location and was part of a committee that planned its creation. Today, Fowler continues working on projects to protect crop diversity.

How Does It Work?

The Svalbard Global Seed Vault's location makes it incredibly secure against natural and human threats. The underground vault is large enough for a huge number of different seed samples.

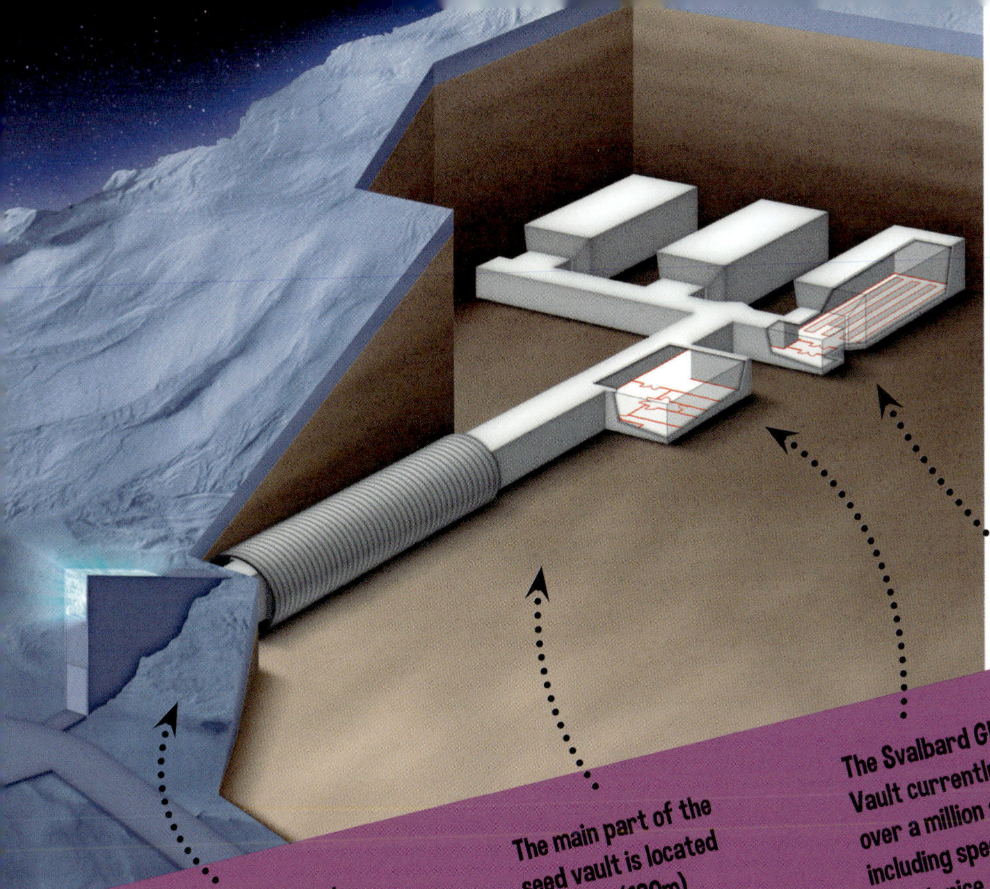

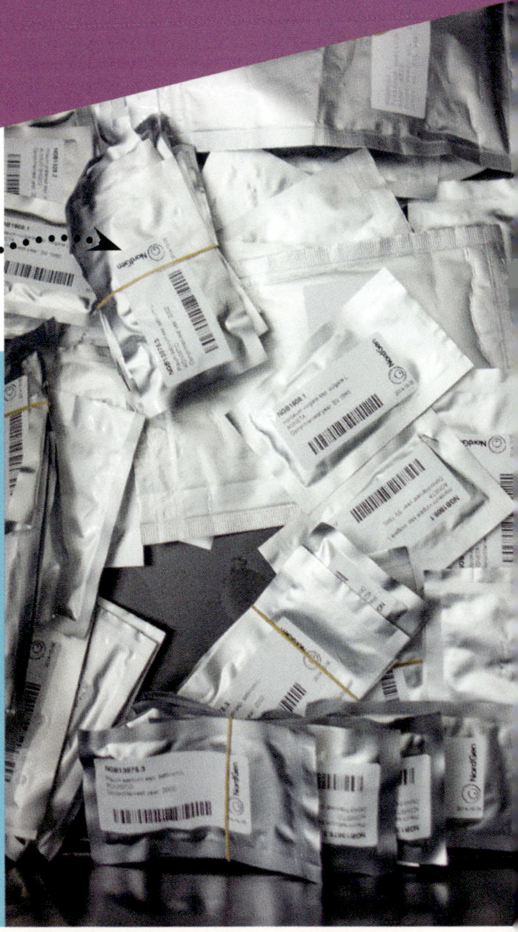

Where Did It Lead?

The seeds stored in the Svalbard Global Seed Vault will be protected for centuries. Its collection is slowly growing as countries send new seed species to be stored there. If global temperatures continue to rise, we may find that some little-used species from the seed banks suit our climate better. These crops may help provide food for communities most affected by climate change.

THINK BIG!

How could you preserve seed samples at home? Design a storage space for seeds. Think about temperature, moisture, light, and protection from animals and diseases.

The Ocean Cleanup

The Ocean Cleanup is a company that develops pioneering technology to remove plastic pollution from oceans and rivers. Their ingenious machines clean up polluted ocean garbage patches and block more plastic from entering the sea.

The Big Idea

Plastic pollution is a huge issue in our oceans. There are an estimated 5 trillion pieces of plastic in the ocean, with an average of 9.3 million tons (8.5 mt) of plastic added every year. These issues inspired the design of the Ocean Cleanup system and Interceptor.

Plastic is very dangerous for ocean wildlife. They often eat it thinking it is food, which can hurt or even kill them.

GENIUS

Boyan Slat (1994–) is a Dutch inventor and entrepreneur. He founded The Ocean Cleanup in 2013 at just 18 years old. Today he is the CEO, but he spends most of his time working on engineering new designs for the company and research.

Around 80 percent of the plastic in the oceans comes from just over 1,000 heavily polluted rivers. The Ocean Cleanup is focusing on placing machines in these rivers to reduce the amount of waste entering the seas.

How Does the Interceptor Work?

The Interceptor machine works like a giant sieve, catching plastic at the mouth of a river where it meets the sea. It can remove 220,462 pounds (100,000 kg) of plastic in just one day! The machine stores the waste it collects until it can be brought to shore by barge for recycling.

How Does the Ocean Cleanup System Work?

The Ocean Cleanup system cleans up garbage patches where plastic clumps together out at sea. The system is made up of a long float that sits on the surface, with a skirt below the water. The skirt traps plastic waste while the float helps the system to move through the garbage patch. The waste is collected by boat and taken for recycling.

The system collects plastic of all sizes, from large pieces down to tiny microplastics that measure just a few millimeters across.

THINK BIG!

The Ocean Cleanup machines work in large spaces such as oceans and river mouths. Can you design a machine that would clean up plastic waste from a smaller body of water, such as a pond or stream? Think about other ways to reduce the machine's environmental impact, such as its energy source.

Desert Sunlight Solar Farm

The Desert Sunlight Solar Farm in California can produce enough electricity to power 160,000 average homes. Its location in the Mojave Desert means that its 8 million solar panels receive around 300 days of sunshine a year!

The Big Idea

Up until the beginning of the 21st century, solar panels were too expensive for large-scale energy generation. New developments in manufacturing helped to bring their price down, which opened up the opportunity for huge solar farms with millions of solar panels.

Generating electricity in solar power plants rather than fossil fuel power plants reduces the amount of CO_2 released into the atmosphere. The amount of CO_2 saved by generating electricity at the Desert Sunlight Solar Farm is equivalent to taking 60,000 cars off the road.

GENIUS

French scientist Edmond Becquerel (1820–1891) was a French scientist who was the first to observe that an electric current was created when certain metals were exposed to light. Other scientists studied this "photovoltaic effect" further, and created the solar cells and panels that we know today.

How Does It Work?

Solar power is a great alternative to fossil fuels. It produces very low greenhouse gas emissions and sunlight is a renewable energy source, meaning it will never run out, unlike fossil fuels.

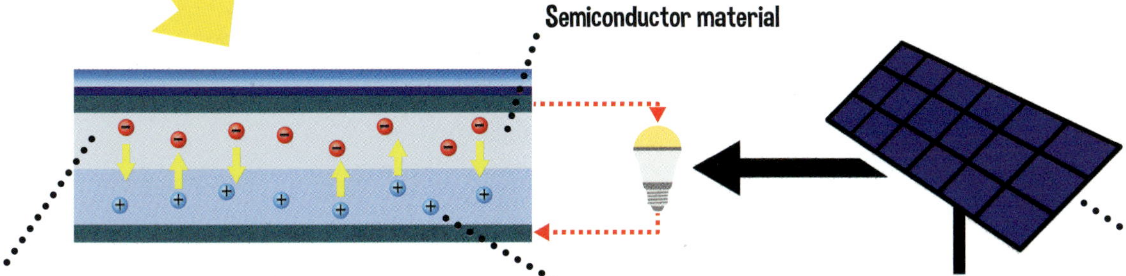

What's Happening Now?

Thanks to an increased interest in green sources of energy, partly due to treaties such as the Paris Agreement (see pages 24–25), many countries are turning to solar power to generate their electricity. It is especially popular in countries with lots of available desert land with the right weather conditions, such as the USA, China, and India.

Some countries are also installing concentrated solar power plants. In these plants, mirrors reflect sunlight onto one central tower. The light energy is converted to heat energy, which powers a steam turbine to generate electricity.

THINK BIG!

The construction of large solar power plants destroys plant and animal habitats. Research how solar power plants affect the desert ecosystem. How could the environmental impact be reduced? Come up with a plan to conserve the natural habitat while still producing electricity.

The Paris Agreement

Climate change is a global issue and working together is key to finding a solution. The Paris Agreement is an international agreement that aims to do just that. Nearly 200 countries within the United Nations have signed the agreement and promised to limit greenhouse gas emissions.

The Big Idea

The aim of the Paris Agreement is to control the rise in global temperature this century. All countries that sign must set goals to limit their greenhouse gas emissions, and report back on their progress every five years. Each country's contribution is different depending on their current level of emissions.

UN representatives after the signing of the Paris Agreement in 2016. Christiana Figueres (see page 25) is on the right.

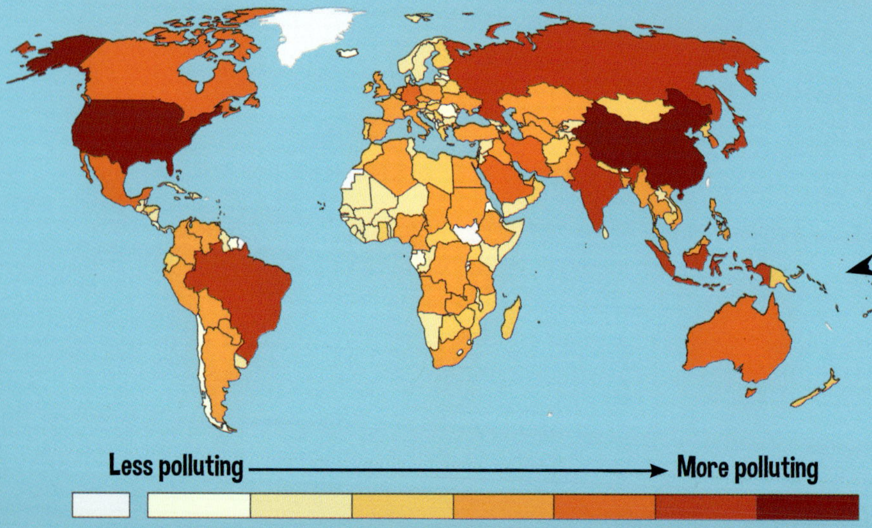

Greenhouse gas emissions vary a lot from country to country. The most polluting countries (shown in red) must try to reduce their emissions the most.

What Is the Plan?

The key to stopping the rise in global temperature is reducing greenhouse gas emissions from power plants, vehicles, and industry as soon as possible. We also need to increase the number of carbon sinks, such as forests, which remove carbon from the atmosphere.

GENIUS

Christiana Figueres (1956–) is a Costa Rican diplomat who has worked on many projects related to climate change and sustainability. She was responsible for the UN's response to global warming in 2016, and led the negotiations that resulted in the Paris Agreement. Previous negotiations had not been successful, but Figueres got the different UN countries to work together.

Where Did It Lead?

Most countries aren't on track to hit the goals that they planned to achieve by 2030. However, some areas with high levels of emissions, such as China, the EU, and the USA, are promising to significantly reduce their emissions later. For example, China has pledged to reach net zero emissions by 2060.

Carbon capture machines that trap carbon dioxide released by power plants could be one way that countries meet the targets of the Paris Agreement.

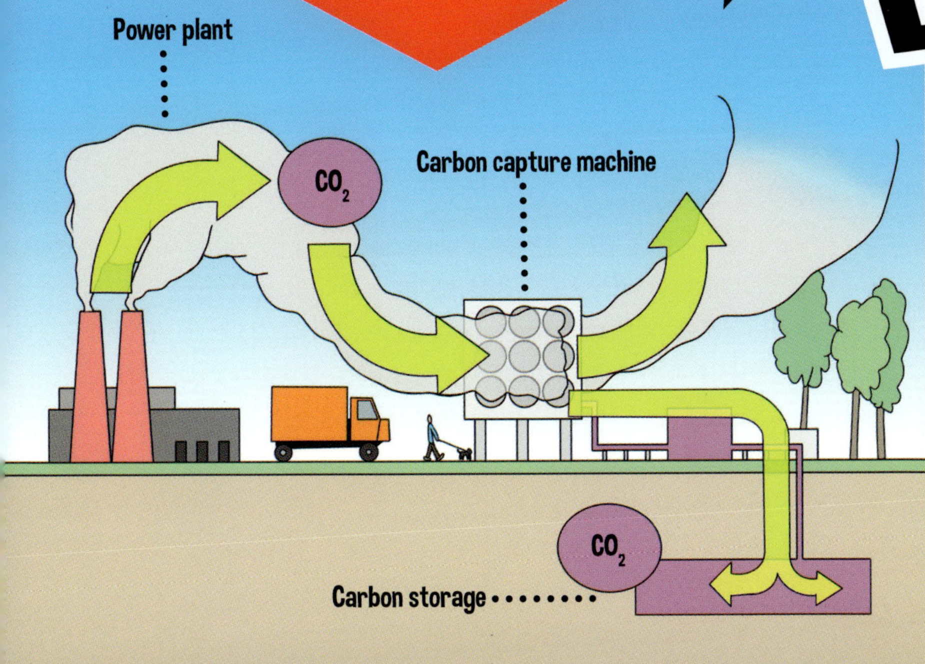

THINK BIG!

Research how carbon sinks work. What methods are currently available and what are their advantages and disadvantages? Present an argument for the method you think would work best in your country.

School Strike for Climate

In 2019, millions of students in hundreds of countries around the world skipped school and took to the streets in climate change demonstrations. They wanted to put pressure on governments to take global warming seriously.

The Big Idea

Shortly after Greta Thunberg's first school strike for climate (see below), young people began to organize protests. They were worried that world leaders weren't prioritizing the environment, and that their generation was going to inherit a planet that couldn't be fixed. Most of these young people weren't old enough to vote, so they used school strikes to make politicians listen to what they had to say.

At the school strike protests, young climate activists addressed crowds about the need to prevent further climate change.

Greta Thunberg was just 15 years old when she started her climate strikes in 2018.

GENIUS

Greta Thunberg (2003–) is a Swedish environmental activist who held the first school strike for climate in 2018. In her first protest, she stood alone outside the Swedish parliament building. Thunberg inspired young people around the world to join her in striking, and it grew into a huge global movement.

Young people created their own posters with inspiring messages at the school climate strikes, including this protest in Sydney, Australia, in 2019.

What Happened?

Events took place in **7,700 cities** around the world throughout 2019.

6 million people protested in the September 2019 climate strike week.

3.5 percent of people in New Zealand took part in the September climate strikes.

'Climate strike' was chosen as the **word of the year** by Collins Dictionary.

People from **212 countries** took part in climate strikes during 2019.

Where Did It Lead?

The school strikes made climate change front-page news around the world. Greta Thunberg and other young activists were given the opportunity to speak at international climate summits, where many leaders voiced their support for the cause. The COVID-19 pandemic paused the protests, but many activists continue to protest online via social media. But so far, the demands of the movement, such as stopping the use of all fossil fuels, have not been met.

THINK BIG!

What action is your school taking against climate change? Form a group with other students and brainstorm different ways of making your school greener. Work with your teachers to make your school as environmentally friendly as possible.

Biodegradable Plastic

Biodegradable plastics could be a solution to the huge amount of plastic pollution that threatens our environment. Rather than filling up landfills and poisoning the water and soil, biodegradable plastics break down naturally and quickly, like organic material.

The Big Idea

Although most plastic can be recycled, it often isn't. Plastic is often covered in food, which means it isn't suitable for recycling. Most plastics end up in landfill sites, where they take many years to break down. When they do break down, they disintegrate into tiny particles called microplastics that are so small they can enter the body and cause health problems in humans and animals.

If we continue to use plastic at the rate we are now, there will be 13.2 billion tons (12 billion mt) of plastic in landfills by 2050.

How Does It Work?

Many biodegradable plastics are bioplastics. They are made from plants, unlike normal plastics, which are made from fossil fuels. In the right conditions, bioplastics will break down into water, biomass, carbon dioxide, or methane, which all exist naturally in the environment.

How Does It Work?

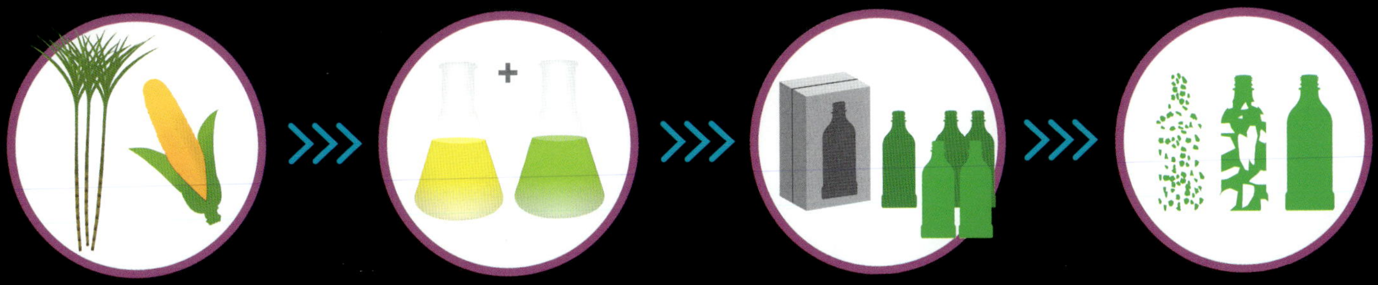

Plants, such as corn and sugar cane, are the main crops used for bioplastics.

The plants are processed and refined to produce the chemical compounds used to create bioplastic.

The bioplastic is formed into the correct shape using molds.

Industrial composters are needed to break down many types of bioplastic.

Where Did It Lead?

Biodegradable plastics are going to become more popular as many countries, such as Canada and the UK, move to ban single-use plastic. However, recycling systems need to be updated so that they have the correct conditions for bioplastics to biodegrade properly. Otherwise, bioplastics will break down slowly and create tiny microplastic particles just like normal plastics.

Some bioplastic plates and cutlery are compostable at home. They can be left to biodegrade with remains of food on them.

THINK BIG!

Choose five food products in your house. How recyclable is their packaging? Remember to look at all the materials and details such as lids and labels. How could you change the packaging to make it totally recyclable?

GENIUS

In 2010, Remy Lucas founded Algopack – a company selling the first bioplastic made from seaweed. Many bioplastics are made from corn, which uses lots of farmland and water. Seaweed grows wild in the sea, so it has less of an environmental impact. Algopack products take just five hours to biodegrade in water and 12 weeks in soil.

Algopack makes plant pots, product packaging and display units from its seaweed bioplastic.

Glossary

activist someone who believes strongly in social or political change, and takes part in action to make this change happen

atmosphere the gases that surround Earth

biodegradable able to decay naturally in a way that does not harm the planet

biodiversity the number and types of plants and animals that live on Earth

biomass dead plants or animals that can be used as fuel

carbon sink something that is able to absorb carbon dioxide from Earth's atmosphere, such as a forest

chlorofluorocarbons (CFCs) chemicals that destroy ozone, previously used in aerosols and other products

deforestation the cutting down of large numbers of trees and the destruction of forests

ecosystem all the living things in an area and their relationships with each other

electron an extremely small piece of matter with a negative electrical charge

emissions the amount of something that is released, for example gas or heat

Industrial Revolution the period of time in which humans started using machines to do work, rather than doing it by hand (c.1760–1900)

meteorologist someone who studies the weather

microplastics extremely small pieces of plastic

organic describes something grown without pesticides or artificial chemicals

ozone layer a layer of ozone gas in the atmosphere that blocks UV light from the Sun

pesticide chemicals used on crops to protect them from being damaged by insects and small animals

photovoltaic effect the process of generating electricity using light

poacher someone who catches and kills animals illegally

renewable something that can be regenerated quickly and easily, and which never runs out

reserve an area of land kept in its natural state where animals are protected

strike a period of time in which people stop working or going to school because they disagree with something or want to make a point

sustainable causing little or no damage to the environment and therefore able to continue for a long time

treaty a formal agreement between countries

United Nations an international organization made up of representatives from different countries, which tries to solve world problems in a peaceful way

Further Information

Books

Endangered Wildlife series by Anita Ganeri (Wayland, 2020)

Energy (Ecographics) by Izzi Howell (Franklin Watts, 2019)

Greta Thunberg and the Climate Crisis by Amy Chapman (Franklin Watts, 2020)

Planting Peace – The Story of Wangari Maathai by Gwendolyn Hooks and Margaux Carpentier (Wayland, 2021)

Sustainable Planet by Anna Claybourne (Franklin Watts, 2022)

Websites

www.earthday.org

Visit the Earth Day website to find events in your local area.

www.nps.gov/yell/learn/photosmultimedia/webcams.htm

Watch live webstreams of Yellowstone National Park.

www.croptrust.org/our-work/svalbard-global-seed-vault/

Learn more about the Svalbard Global Seed Vault.

theoceancleanup.com/oceans/

Learn more about the Ocean Cleanup and its machines that remove plastic from oceans and rivers.

Index